SEE ME, SEE

John Pepper

Illustrated by Rowel Friers

BLACKSTAFF PRESS

Published by Blackstaff Press Limited, 255A Upper Newtownards Road, Belfast BT4 3JF.

ISBN 0 85640 156 0

Printed in Northern Ireland by The Northern Whig Ltd.

Contents

'It's going to bed that keeps me on my feet.'

It is dangerously easy to fall into the trap of forming a judgment about a community by hearsay, even by appearances. Not until the people who live in it are heard talking can it be said that anything approaching a realistic portrait of them be drawn.

The truth is that until they open their mouths, people are to a great extent a closed book. From Biblical times speech has been the great give-away.

It is thus arguable that only when the everyday talk of Ulster is set down in evidence that its character can be properly and accurately assessed.

It was in the buses, the shopping queues, in the streets, in the black taxis and around the firesides of Northern Ireland that the utterances here put on record were heard. They reflect so strikingly and in their own style an outlook, a philosophy, an attitude, that I am convinced it would be a pity if they were allowed to go with the wind.

Any community in which it is possible to hear day and daily such statements as:

'When I get rid of this leg of mine I'll walk round to see you.'

'See me, my feet were that sore pounding round the shops that I went and got my hair done.'

'A budgie ties you down when you want to get away.'

'It's going to bed that keeps me on my feet,'

must at least be said to have its own vibrant touch when it comes to the lively use of language.

It is for these reasons that I have put together this fresh collection of examples of Ulster speech. It is as much as anything else to emphasise that *What a Thing to Say* really only skimmed the surface.

John Pepper

What the Experts Say

'The Northern Irish voice is quick, high-pitched, and emphatic, with an upward turn at the end of a sentence, so quick, indeed, that you must run to hear it. A Belfastman laughs heartily at himself; the Dubliner laughs only at other people.'

St John Ervine, Ulster author and playwright.

'Northern Ireland was fortunate to acquire its English during the uninhibited Elizabethan period because Elizabethans became eloquent before they became grammatical.'

Professor John Braidwood, Head of the Department of English, Queen's University, Belfast.

'The Ulster way of speech is the least attractive, least melodious, nay the ugliest of all the branches of the English language.'

Charles C. Russell in a book published in 1910.

'Conversation in Ulster is a sharp, quick, metallic clatter compared with the rich drawled-out brogue of the South and the musical accent of the refined Dubliner.'

Rev. W. McMordie of Kilkeel, in a book published in 1890 condemning the 'debasement of the noble English language in Ulster.'

'It behoves us to look at our Ps and Qs and avoid using such expressions as Proddisin for Protestant and umberella for umbrella.'

David Patterson in *The Provincialisms of Belfast Pointed out and Corrected*, published in 1860.

'The Northern Irish are, on the whole, an extremely unattractive group of people. They are dour, troublesome and truculent, quarrelsome, bigoted and rough. Charmlessness is their main characteristic and humourlessness their middle name.'

Mary Kenny, Irish author.

'See me? I feel like a tossed bed.'

A fairly reliable method of indicating in Roman times that you were a man with a message was to use the phrase, 'Lend me your ears.' It could be said to be a conversational Appian Way equivalent of 'Red Eye Calling Harelip.'

In Northern Ireland a simpler oratorical convention is used as an opening gambit. It consists merely of launching into the disclosure, pronouncement, or confession by saying 'See me?'

The practice is not exclusive to Ulster but has been adopted there on such a scale that it has acquired a dimension of its own.

The words can be the prelude to a simple statement of fact, as in the case of the bus passenger who told his companion, 'See me? I can't stand soft hard-boiled eggs over a salad.'

The speaker's life-style can be effectively conveyed with the help of the two magic words.

'See me? I could just live on dip.'

'See me? I bought a piece of steak last week and the jaws of hell couldn't eat it.'

'See me? I'm dying about tea you can stand on.'

A sense of modesty at one's appearance can be neatly indicated: 'See me? I feel like a tossed bed.'

Omit the two words and the statement somehow develops a flavour of boastfulness alien to the Ulster character. Without them the confidences which follow would appear presumptuous, as if they were being thrust down the listener's throat, regardless.

'See me? I wouldn't hurt a fly but one of these days I'm going to thump the lining out of that brother-in-law of mine.'

'See me? I wouldn't ate an egg from a duck that woman would rear.'

'See me? I can't be bothered with television ever since they stopped *Dr Finlay's Bookcase*.'

'See me? I can't do it with my head but I could do it with a pencil.'

Thick and fast the revelations heralded in this fashion fly through the Ulster air.

'See me? I'd just love a wee two-storey bungalow to live in.'

'See me? I never knew it was you till I looked at you.'

'See me? I haven't supped since yesterday. Nothing will lie on my stomach.'

'See me? I'm not at myself. I haven't drawn breath this fortnight.'

'See me? The dentist told me to hold on while he nearly pulled the head off me. What do you think he meant?'

'See me? I told the breadman to give me three of them sliced loaves. I find them easier to cut.'

'See me? My ones don't like fish from the sea. They'd rather have it from the shop.'

Behind the usage there is often a desire simply to start the conversational ball rolling, come what may; an urge to have a chat, to gossip.

'See me? Sure a banana would kill me, so it would.'

'See me? I'm married to the divil's sister.'

But it is only a stranger who would think it was a non sequitur when told, 'See me? My feet were that sore pounding round the shops that I went and got my hair done.'

The convention has developed interesting variations. For example, it is possible to hear, 'See me? See my feet? They get awful dirty cleaning.'

Another runs 'Here's me. Still Johnny the boatman.' This indicates the speaker's disenchantment that promotion should have again passed him by.

Another variant was adopted by the man who was having the worst of an argument with his wife and finally burst out, 'See you? See your mother?' as if nothing more had to be said.

'See her?' is usually resorted to when a damaging comment is intended.

'See her? She could look through a keyhole with both eyes.'

'See her? She would steal your glass eye and say you could see better without it.'

'See her? She's as hard to look at as the south side of an apple tree.'

'See her? There's not the like of her within the ringing of a bell.'

'See her? I've told that wee girl a thousand times not to exaggerate.'

'See her? She's that bitter she says at you whatever comes to her stomach.'

'See her? The back of her heels is always boggin'.'

When it comes to 'See him?' the examples are no less comprehensive, often no less blistering.

'See him? He fell into that farm of his.' This indicates envy of the man's inheritance.

'See him? I asked him if he had washed his face and he said he had but his ma always told him it dries a bad colour.'

'See him? You wouldn't have him on the behind of your britches.'

'See him? He couldn't drive a barra straight up a pritta sheugh.'

There are always the exceptions to every rule, of course.

'See him? He'd pass for a gentleman even in his bare pelt.'

There are occasions when the two words are apt to induce the retort, 'Of course I see you,' but this will put the speaker only momentarily off his or her stride.

The device embraces all members of the family. None is immune.

'He has as much use for a wife as a duck for an umbrella.'

'See granny? She always says she likes two cups of tea in her lap before lying down.'

'See grandpa? He snores all night and half the day like a bog eel.'

'See my Aunt Lizzie? She says there's far less tarmacadam in them mental fegs.'

'See my wee lad? He had eight sandwiches, fourteen buns, and six cups of tea at the party and he told me he could have had his fill if he had liked.'

'See my brother-in-law? He has a mouth like a butcher's cupboard. It won't shut for bones.'

'See my Uncle Andy? He has as much call for a wife as a duck has for an umbrella.'

'See my cousin Elly? She's as odd as two's evens.'

Places as well as people can be roped in — and constantly are.

'See her house? She's that fussy you daren't open your mouth in it in case your breath shows on the mirrors.'

'See this place? It's two blankets colder than anywhere else.'

'See Spain? Nobody could eat thon food they give you.'

'See the boarding house we stayed in? I didn't get a wink of sleep at night for the toilet striking the hour every five minutes.'

'See my garden? It has me bent double fighting the weeds.'

'See my car? It's using petrol by the square yard so it is.'

The idea of indicating that you are about to give utterance takes other forms as well, to be used according to taste or mood.

'Funny enough' has spread from the mainland and, with refinements, is now part and parcel of the Ulster idiom.

'Funny enough, he died the same day as his wife.'

'Funny enough, the best man got putrid at his wedding.'

'Funny enough, his oul lad was also a bit of a comedian.'

'Funny enough, he fell and broke his leg going to see a sick uncle in hospital.'

'Funny enough, wee Willie tuk out the pram and, funny enough, he cowped it. But the wain wasnae in it, funny enough.'

Basically all the openings I have mentioned are little more than variations of the international 'Get this'. They serve the same purpose but have been given the stamp of a home product and thus acquire their own value.

'I'll walk round to see you when I get rid of this leg of mine.'

Listen to everyday Ulster speech and, unless you know the language, the possession of physical qualities little short of the acrobatic seems constantly to be implied. The place is made to sound as if it is over-run by contortionists.

You would be looked on as retarded, for example, if you got the idea that an amputation was pending if you heard the statement, 'I'll walk round to see you when I get rid of this leg of mine.'

Similarly the woman who confided, 'I rest in bed as much as I can for I find it keeps me on my feet' would almost seem to be indicating that she had serious levitation problems.

If you are told, 'I have another head this morning,' it falls nearly into the pattern which includes, 'I've been trying to get rid of my head all morning,' and the common lament, 'It's a pity of that fella. His head's gone.'

The familiar 'Open the window and throw out your chest' is only the beginning in Ulster. The process is taken a great deal further.

'I saw his face on the Ormeau Road' is an illustration, as is the comment of the office cleaner, complimented on the spotless condition of the floor she had just polished, 'I always use my head when I'm doing it.'

What happens when she complains 'My head's away this morning' is a matter for speculation.

'I haven't a head that would take me to the corner' introduces a further element into the syndrome. However, a compliment is clearly meant if you are told, 'You have a quare head on you.'

The woman who suffered from spasmodic headaches put it in her own style with the words, 'It would drive you dimented. You nivver know the minute when the oul head starts splittin', then it stops. It's like a bap in a baker's cart. Here one minute and away the next.'

Constantly there is inescapable evidence that exceptional physical attributes are indigenous to the place, that it is crammed with people who have two heads, several arms, exceptional stomachs, detachable limbs.

One example is provided by the householder who was pointing out that his house had been burgled and said, 'They broke into my back, so they did.'

And what could the uninitiated make of the words a woman addressed to a neighbour 'I saw her walking along the side of the City Hall with her broken arm'?

'See him there?' a Belfastman will say, and to the inquiry, 'Who?' will immediately answer, 'Him with his back to you, facing you.'

Listen to the parental complaint, 'I keep telling the child to eat his dinner but it just goes in one ear and out the other' and there would appear to be grounds for assuming that all these Ulster peculiarities have been there since infancy.

A Limavady woman complained to her doctor, 'You gave me a right leg last week,' leaving herself open to the suggestion that if only it had been a *left* leg all would have been well.

A pianist's message to the organiser of a church concert, explaining why she was unable to get to the performance, said simply, 'I can't play with my feet.' It did not mean she had out of the ordinary musical talents, just that she had to go to hospital with swollen toes.

If her absence from, say, a wine-tasting gathering had been due to the same cause, presumably she would have sent word, 'I can't drink with my feet.'

It was a woman who had been to her dentist to have several painful extractions who excused herself from proposing a vote of thanks at a Co. Antrim sale of work by intimating, 'I can't speak with my mouth.'

She would doubtless have been quite at home with the woman who commented during a severe spell of frost, 'It was hard to hold your feet this morning.'

The words of the man from Maghera who insisted, 'You can't beat soda farls. Sure I learned to walk on sodas,' are guaranteed to create a distinct interest in his gait.

The invitation, 'Come round some night when you're staying in,' has its own tones of abnormality, as in the case of the man who was told the bus he wanted had just left and that it would be some time before the next one, 'That's all right, he replied, 'I'll just walk on while I'm waiting.'

The query, 'Where were you going that time I saw you coming back?' would not cause any raised eyebrows in Ulster. It belongs to the same class of convoluted speech as, 'If you're not in I'll know you're away.'

There aren't many communities where an understanding look would follow the statement, 'That fella has drunk three farms, so he has.' Only an outsider would fail to grasp right away that it summed up the sad story of an alcoholic.

This also applies to the complaint of the shopper buying a pair of trousers for a child, was asked what size, and said, 'It's awful hard to carry the children's legs in your head.'

Unusual digestive abilities are far from being hinted at by the harassed Banbridge housewife who lamented, 'Do you know this? If I ate the drawers

I couldn't find the bread-knife.'

In a similar vein is the wail, 'My man's in bed with his kidneys and d'ye know why? He threw aff a pullover.'

The woman who said, 'I can't get rid of my stomach,' further emphasises the degree to which Ulster people never really expect to be taken literally.

But then it would be a much duller place if they did. It would be a sad day indeed if no one ever heard the explanation of the woman whose son had emigrated to Canada, was asked when he had last been home, and said, 'The last time was before he went.'

It would be no less a deprivation never to have heard the words of the woman, when told by a friend who had gone on a tourist flight to Toronto and was the victim of a street accident, 'Imagine going all that distance to be knocked down.'

It would be just as regrettable to be robbed of the kind of pronouncement made about an ailing husband, 'He went straight to bed last night bent in two.'

'Mind you, I was fairly dropped on.'

Whatever may be said of Ulster people's ways no one can accuse them of being spendthrifts in speech. They have a devout belief in the principle of sticking to the same word for as many uses as possible.

Whether or not this can be put down to laziness, it produces some striking examples of overworking, especially with the word 'on', which has a thousand and one deployments. Few two-letter words are exploited with such persistence.

By asking 'Have you the time on you?' an Ulsterman could be trying to discover the exact time but could also be seeking to establish if you are too busy to tackle a task he has in mind.

'Have you a match on you?' is more straightforward, but momentary domestic confusion was caused when a new charwoman inquired of her employer, 'Have you a bucket on you?'

It will be said of a couple whose marriage is heading for the rocks, 'I've been told they don't get on,' while a small boy will counsel a playmate to keep mum about some mischief in which they have been involved, 'Don't you be lettin' on about it.'

A girl will tell a playmate with whom she has quarrelled, 'I'm not on with you.'

'He took it on himself' will be applied to someone who has assumed authority without particular justification.

There is all the warmth in the world behind the invitation to a caller, 'Come on on in.'

Someone showing their age will have it said of them, 'He's getting on,' and a person who tends to nag will risk the rebuke, 'I wish you wouldn't keep on about it.'

'You're having me on' shows that the speaker knows an attempt is being made to pull his leg.

An ailing woman will say, 'I've been put on tablets again.'

Anyone given the warning, 'I'll put the dog on you' will be well advised to make themselves scarce. If it was a threat that came as a surprise the comment may be made, 'I was fairly dropped on over it.'

The advice 'Catch yourself on' is usually given when someone oversteps the mark.

'Come round and see us if you have nothing on' should not be considered an invitation to an orgy.

Tribute will be paid to someone who dresses neatly, 'He's awful well put on,' while the words, 'He's gettin' on for ninety' clearly indicate that the march of time is taking its toll.

'He's on the bottle again' tells its own story of the life style of a man who enjoys a dram. It is generally used by a stiffly religious person of someone with a happy-go-lucky philosophy. The same approach will be behind the comment, 'He had a drop or two on him at the time.' Similarly, 'He's well on' has the frigid, condemnatory flavour of a charge of having had one too many.

'He's waiting on' is a way of indicating that someone is on his deathbed. The next step brings the remark, 'He has passed on.'

The impression might be given that I am keeping *on* unduly about this Ulster characteristic but the truth is that it doesn't end there. I have only scratched the surface.

And to emphasise just how *on*-ward the people are, mention might be made of their insistence in substituting 'on' for 'in' at every opportunity.

This is responsible for such variations as:

'It is my own onaided work.'

'That fella's very onbusinesslike.'

'The man was lying on the ground onconscious.'

'The envelope was onopened.'

'I thought the situation was very ondesirable.'

'He's on the bureau because he's onemployed.'

'She's very onselfish.'

A man with 'a right pair of hands'.

'The wee lady was very onruly.'

What Ulster would do without the simple but useful little preposition it is hard to say. If they were to be deprived of it they would probably feel they were being 'put up*on*'.

Oddly enough 'off' has its own element of enthusiastic usage.

A woman suffering from what is known as a 'heaving stomach' will ask the chemist for, 'A bottle to stop me from feeling off colour.'

An employee can be 'told off' for indifferent attention to his duties, and a young woman who has tired of an admirer will say, 'I've gone off him.' If he is replaced in double quick time by someone else it will be said, 'She got off with him.'

Meat or meat pies, besides milk, can be 'off' and are liable to be the cause of people being 'off' work.

And it could well be that by now the reader has reached the stage of murmuring impatiently, 'For goodness sake knock if off.'

A further spot on the list of words with a manifold use is the handy 'right'.

'We've got a right one here' probably owes its frequent usage to television, but those people denounced as 'a right quilt', 'a right gulpin', 'a right skitter', or 'a right so-and-so' are not usually those held in the highest regard.

The man with 'a right pair of hands' is not necessarily ambidexterous, nor is 'a right speaker' necessarily a Conservative.

'It was a right feed' is a testimonial to an excellent meal, just as 'It's a right day for sneddin' turnips' describes perfect weather on the farm.

'She's right'n bad' may sound as if the lady's signature was illegible, but it is only the uninformed who would fail to be aware that what was meant was that the lady was 'in bed with the doctor'.

'Rightly', of course, runs the word close in everyday speech.

'He was rightly' describes someone who has been celebrating over-wisely, but 'He's rightly' can also indicate recovery from illness.

'He's rightly on' is usually applied to a man of advanced age while the businessman who is 'doing rightly' is clearly keeping bankruptcy successfully at bay.

There are many occasions when it would seem that Ulster people suffer from word shortage to a chronic degree.

This is particularly so if you hear the recital, 'I got up, got my breakfast, got the car out, got in, got to the office, got on with my work, got into trouble with the boss, got my notice, got the message, got fed up, got into an argument, got plastered, got sick, got home, got the wife out of her bed, got told enough, and got to my bed.'

The conclusion would appear to be that there is a lot to be said of the proposal that 'got' is a word to be got rid of.

'A budgie ties you down terribly if you want to get away.'

It is claimed that if a particular dialect is not easily understood by an outsider it is because of the accent rather than the indifferent grammar.

Even to Ulster ears the Yorkshireman's saying, 'Ez nak't ez a graavsteen' is not instantly clear. When an Ulsterman speaks, however, an additional complication is introduced.

'Would you like a cup of tea for a drink?' a visitor will be asked. It may sound an absurd question but it is put like that to emphasise that you are being offered something to quench your thirst, not tea accompanied by something to eat. The point is that you are not being invited to a meal.

There is logic of a sort — though not instantly apparent to the outsider — in the comment of a police officer after bringing to safety a climber who had clung to a ledge until rescue came, 'If he hadn't stayed where he was he would still have been there.'

It is not unlike the approach demonstrated by the statement about the chronic school truant, 'Some days he wasn't there for a week.'

This gift for introducing complications that have nothing to do with accent takes many forms.

A resident in a seaside town watched a boat leave on a trip round the bay and was heard to murmur, 'There's not many on her tonight but them that is has the best seats.'

No less unusual is the philosophy reflected in the Belfastman's pronouncement, 'I just couldn't be bothered with a budgie. It ties you down terribly if you want to get away.'

The approach covers all kinds of situations. A woman about to cross a Belfast street assured her companion, 'So long as you're on the crossing when they hit you, you're entitled to compensation.'

If the sense is sometimes difficult to follow it should be remembered that the Ulster idiom is peppered with expressions that are perfect examples of Elizabethan usage.

The phrase 'That'll learn you' shows the verb being used to indicate 'That will teach you a lesson to be more careful next time.' It is only one of the many examples of Elizabethan English still to be heard.

A youngster who had shone in a geography class at school was asked by the teacher, 'Did your mother learn you?'

'No,' he replied, 'It was my da, mostly after tea if I wasn't in bed.'

It is important to listen attentively in Ulster. This was brought home to the visitor who was told, 'I'd make you a cup of tea only the teapot hasn't been itself the whole day.' It is the kind of statement that can cause utter bewilderment if only half-heard.

The same confusion can be created by the words of the guest as she watched a cup of tea being poured for her, 'Just give me what you would know, for I've been drinking tea the whole morning.'

A husband's instruction to his wife on finishing his breakfast, 'Wud ye throw the teapot down the toilet,' can bring a startled reaction to the uninitiated, just as can the comment at a crowded lecture, 'If only there weren't so many people here they could get more in.'

An English tourist saw a group round a man who had collapsed in the street, was told the ambulance had been called, and asked, 'What happened to him?' He was told, 'We're waiting for him to come till,' and was left little the wiser.

A touch of subtlety is not readily grasped in the reply of the resident of an Ulster country town, the scene of several sectarian clashes, when asked if there had been any improvement in the atmosphere.

'Ach,' he said, 'we get on all right now. We clod at each other now and then but that's about all.'

Any tendency towards boastfulness is given appropriate treatment, no nonsense about it, as in:

'I flew over from London to save time.'

'It musta been awful sore on your armpits over the Isle of Man.'

The farmer who said to have been 'dandering along the road on his bacon rind soles' sounds a real oddity until it is realised that crepe soles were meant. There is a distinct resemblance.

The statement joins the category of the unexpected resorted to by the woman who said, 'I had a brother who was at sea for a while but he just couldn't stick it because he couldn't go to the corner for the paper every morning.'

And there is its own flavour of word power about the comment made to a woman who had developed a cheek rash, 'If you don't watch out that face'll cripple you for life.'

Ulster people are generally cautious when questioned. It is considered unwise to commit yourself.

This tendency was demonstrated by the woman who had a sister in

Canada and was asked how long she had been away.

'Ach, about ten years,' was the answer, 'but she doesn't know yet whether she'll stay.'

On the other hand there is no hesitancy about providing the information when a Co. Down woman was being questioned during a radio phone-in.

Ashed was she married she replied, 'Seven years.'

Then came the question, 'How many children have you?'

'Two.'

'And what are they?' asked the interviewer, seeking to establish if they were a boy and a girl.

'They're both Protestants,' he was told.

There is its own air of swift assessment about the summing up by a Belfast security man who had watched a cat dodge the wheels of a bus by a hairsbreadth, 'If thon cat hadda been a dog it wudda been a dead duck.'

'I thought I was sent for' does not imply the receipt of an urgent call to an important meeting. It conveys nothing more than that the speaker had a narrow escape, usually on the road.

'Hard cheese' is not a criticism confined to the dinner table. It is the equivalent of 'Hard luck'. Sometimes 'Hardy dough' will be murmured. This serves the same purpose.

The invitation, 'Would you like a taste?' should make the visitor to Ulster take care. It is not a suggestion that he should try out whatever is on offer, but an invitation to have a cup of tea or coffee, perhaps a drink of orange juice, maybe even a glass of Scotch.

This lack of local knowledge spelt trouble for a dinner party guest from England who was asked if he would like a second helping.

'Thank you,' he said, and waited in vain for his plate to be refilled, unaware that his reply was taken to mean, 'No thank you.'

Similar confusion faced the guest who paid no attention when his neighbour said, 'Thank you for the salt.' The words were repeated a second time, then a third, until finally he was given a firm nudge in the ribs and told, 'Would you for ever pass my mother the salt?'

A philosophy no less complicated was probably to blame for the comment of the County Down woman who confided to a friend about a family living in a nearby development' 'The truth is that they're clean dirty. It's all you could say about them.'

Thus the unexpected keeps bobbing up in Ulster speech.

During an election a woman was asked if she had voted and replied, 'Ach, I didn't bother. Sure they'll get in anyway.'

And it takes some moments' thought to appreciate the comment sparked off by a woman shopper who had burrowed her way through a solid crush of of people, turned to apologise to the owner of a basket she had almost upset, apologised, and was told, 'Next time you say you're sorry get your photo taken.'

'Would you like some jube-jubes for your ears?

Ulster people, when they go abroad, take their identity with them. It is not something to be left behind, no matter how far they travel. Their style of life, their speech, their outlook are not things to be lightly discarded to suit new surroundings.

Only a Belfastman, for example, could have asked the question which flummoxed those who overheard it on a Belfast-London plane.

An English passenger wanted a cigarette, discovered he was in the non-smoking section of the aircraft, and asked the hostess if he could move. She told him to follow her.

The plane was then approximately half-way over the Irish Sea, flying at an altitude of around 15,000 feet, and the traveller was about to sit down and light up, when the man in the next seat looked up at him and asked wonderingly, 'Have you just got on?'

The two men started chatting and the Belfastman soon reached the stage of producing snaps of his family. The Englishman followed suit and displayed a shot taken in Devon. It showed him walking along a country lane with two small dogs at his heels.

'They're lovely wee animals,' the Belfastman said.

'Actually they're Jack Russels,' it was pointed out.

'That a fact?' said the Belfastman. 'I thought they were your own.'

Another English traveller, flying back to London after a Belfast business trip, had no less daunting an experience.

As the plane was taking off, rather bumpily, the woman in the seat alongside nudged him gently, gestured to him with a small paper bag, and asked hospitably, 'Would you like some jube-jubes for your ears?'

This gift for taking Ulster homeliness along was also encountered by a passenger on a jet flight from Montreal to Belfast.

The cooling system on the aircraft had developed a fault and the pilot announced that in the interest of everyone's comfort drinks would be served free.

Beside the traveller was the inevitable Ulsterwoman, returning home after a visit to relatives, who took full advantage of the invitation and soon had consumed her sixth can of Coke.

Before long they had their predictable effect. The plane was hurtling through the clouds at a speed of approximately 500 mph, thirty to forty thousand feet above the wide Atlantic, when she struggled to her feet and whispered to the startled fellow passenger, 'Excuse me. I hafta go to the yard.'

Air travel somehow manages to conflict with Ulster's reputation as a place where feet are kept firmly on the ground.

A Larne woman had completed the necessary form-filling for an insurance policy on the life of her husband. When the final details had been filled in she asked, 'Are you sure now that everything has been taken care of, that it will be all right if anything should happen? You're sure?'

'Missus,' was the confident reply. 'If your husband dropped dead this minute you'd be flying.'

I was told of one Ulsterwoman travelling from Heathrow who was taking her seat in the plane when the woman about to sit down beside her said accusingly, 'You didn't pick a very good seat, did you?'

She blinked in surprise and was soon enlightened when the woman said, 'I picked you to travel with when we were standing at the airport. I always pick somebody to travel with. I saw you. Didn't you see me?'

There was a pause in the chat as the aircraft finally took off but the lady was soon in full flow again.

'I've been visiting my son,' she explained. 'I brought a deck chair back with me but there's no extra charge for it because I just tied it on to my suitcase with a bit of cord.'

The comment of the lady's erstwhile companion was, 'As a solution to the problem of travelling alone who but an Ulsterwoman would come up with this approach? If I ever hear of her again she's welcome to another trip.'

Northern Ireland warmth comes to the surface just as readily in a jumbo jet as in the bus to Aughnacloy. The person in the seat alongside is someone to talk to, a friendly soul until they are shown to be otherwise.

Typifying this companionable instinct was the assurance of the Belfastman to the worried woman passenger during a bumpy landing at Aldergrove, 'It's okay, missus. Everything's all right. We're over the ramps. We can land now.'

It was in a Liverpool to London train that a woman from Coleraine took the breath away from her reserved fellow-passenger by an almost non-stop discussion about her relatives and their peculiarities. It concluded, 'Muncle Jimmy — he was a powerful man. Powerful. His only trouble was that he

'It's the cowl I'm starving with, not hunger.'

had bad feet. Never stopped talking about his bunions. There wasn't anything Doctor Scholl made Muncle Jimmy didn't buy. The house was coming down with the stuff he bought for his feet. The one thing about Muncle, though, was that he was a terrible argier. Terrible. He argied on me once that a good pigeon could fly the 'Clantic if it had a coupla landing places in between. Imagine that.'

The lady's bewildered listener could do little else but try frantically to work it all out. She did not find it easy. It was no help that the Coleraine lady kept introducing new relations. Before long 'Muncle Jimmy' was joined by 'Arjoe', another member of the family.

'Arjoe's just like one of them cement mixers,' came the revelation. 'Throw anything intil him, 'specially it its a wheen of spuds, and he's as happy as Larry. I'll never forget when he was wee. I usta tell him to go out intil the garden and play himself. I wud tell him if I looked out and he wasn't there I'd bring him in but damn the heed did he pay me.'

She had other disclosures. Clearly she had enough of them to have lasted for a journey three times the length of that from Liverpool to London.

'There was the time I went to the Isle of Man on the steamer. God but it was cowl. I sat for hours in my hat and coat and when a steward came up to me I told him I was starving so I was. So he went away and brought me tea and biscuits on a wee tray. You should have seen the look I gave him. "You're a stupa ijit," I told him, "It's the cowl I'm starving with," I said, "not hunger."'

There is a strong likelihood that the woman would have behaved little differently from the Ulsterwoman on a visit to members of her family who had emigrated to America. She decided to pay a surprise call on a former neighbour she hadn't seen for more than twenty years and was living in the area.

She walked up to the ex-neighbour's door and when it was opened exclaimed, 'How're ye Alice?'

Without a pause there was the reply, 'How're ye Lizzie?'

The same kind of casual treatment of new surroundings marked the request of the Ulsterman at a London dinner. Completely unabashed by the luxurious surroundings at the banquet, the impressive menu, and the distinguished guests, he nudged the man beside him and said in a voice well above a confidential whisper. 'Wudya tell the fella at the end there to pass up the baskit with the wee holes in it?'

He had his eye on another roll — and got it.

'I always thought she had a funny laugh.'

Take a seat in a bus going through almost any part of Northern Ireland and it will be found that the air is thick with lively speech and colourful revelations. Listen — and you are almost made to feel like one of the family.

Unless politics are being discussed there is usually a reluctance to speak in whispers. People don't mind being overheard. The rewards are thus all the greater for those who delight in the capture of intriguing fragments of dialogue, the kind that flutter through the air like invisible butterflies.

Two young women, for example, discuss a dance attended by one of them. She could hardly be described as Miss Universe material.

'Wur ye lifted?'

'The fellas weren't up to much.'

'But wur ye lifted? Dint anybody ast ye if ye wanted a birl?'

'Ach they did.'

'Wur they any good?'

'Ach sure, I wudna be bothered with any one of them. Some of them danced as if they'd still got their gum boots on.'

Two elderly ladies whose opinions of their circle of friends were consistently critical cosily exchange views:

'Her? I knew she was a poultice the minute I set eyes on her.'

'Me too. Between you and me and the wall I always thought she had a funny laugh.'

'A puke. Never has a good word to say of anybody.'

'It's not a word of a lie. And with all due respects to that man of hers, I never thought he was up to much.'

'Know what I'm going to tell you? What you say is the God's honest truth.'

Two workmen, both pipe smokers, talk between puffs:

'I see Davy's drivin' her the night. Davy always gets a move on.'

'Davy's the boy. He was telling me he looked in to see that oul aunt of his last week and she ast him if he'd like a cuppa tea. "Nivver borr," he says to her, trying to be polite like, and d'ye know this? The bloody woman nivver borrered.

'Shows ye.'

'Right enough. No doubt about it, Davy the driver's going like the hammers.'

'Funny thing, though. I've often thought about it. Isn't it funny the way the bus goes twice as fast when you're runnin' after it as when you're in it.'

'It's not a word of a lie.'

Both the 'D'ye mind?' and 'Jamember' forms of prelude are usually a signal that interesting material is on its way.

'I was thinking, Andy. D'ye mind the time we used to get into the pitchers with a jampot?'

'Many's the jampot I pinched outa me ma's kitchen. Many's the one.'

'Them wus the days, Andy. Every time I luk at television it makes me think that begod they put more life intil their dyin' in them oul cowboy pitchers. Far more.'

'You're right there. I was thinking. Jamember the chuckers out they used to have? Jamember?'

''Member well, Andy. Walked up and down the passage wi' a long pole to keep the childer from misbehavin' themselves.'

'That's right. An' one wud shine his flashlamp an' call out "Show us yir hands."'

'Mind him well, Andy. Do indeed.'

The confidences can embrace every conceivable subject — the weather, ill health, marital relations, family weaknesses, the price of drink, childhood. Nothing is too trivial.

'They're saying Maggie's girl's getting married the morrow. Did you hear anything?'

'You're right. The marra's the day.'

Listen to the chatty little woman in the black raincoat, in her lap a string bag containing a packet of shredded wheat, a sliced loaf, a bunch of bananas and a toilet roll:

'Andy was goin' out the other night and you'd have thought he was headin' for Buckingham Palace for a medal he was that fussy.'

'Sure, Andy always is a tidy wee man.'

'Tidy my backside, Lilian. He called me once till the fut of the stairs, he called me twice, and he called me three times. It was all because he said he cudn't fine the tie he wanted. I tole him straight I'd had enough. I sez to him I said, right out, "I'll go up myself an' fine yir oul tie for ye and wrap it round yir thrapple."'

A slim woman, wearing glasses, her mouth prim, has an intent listener in the younger woman beside her:

'The time we went to Spain last year it was a quare geg. We went for the Twelfth fortnight. The crush at the customs was terbil. You have no idea. Me and Robert got separated.'

'Musta been awful for you.'

'When I saw him again he was in a right tizzy so he was. You have no idea. Them customs men, he said. He was livid. Them bastards made me cowp my attachey case on the bench.'

'You don't say. Mind you I can understand his feelings. My sister Harriet, she was in Spain last year too. Benidorm.'

'Benidorm's nice.'

'Out of this world. She said it was stickin' out. Anyway there was this day on the beach.'

'The beaches are nice.'

'Anyway there was this girl. A blonde. Luked like a film star, Harriet said. Dignified, like. And there was this fella. Kept cloddin' wee pebbles at her. You know, tryin' to gett aff?'

'You could take your dead end at some of them.'

'Anyway it got to the stage that she couldn't stand any more of it, Harriet said. It was gettin' to be too much of a good thing. So the girl turns round and gives the fella a luk. Then she draws herself up and says, "Away outa that, ye wee skitter." Harriet said she could hardly credit that the girl had come from this part of the world. It give her a right shock.'

At the back of the bus, hear the man with the thin moustache. It could probably be said of him, 'He could take a drink.' He and his companion look as if it was some time since they were offered refreshment — at least an hour.

'Bob the barman. You know Bob?'

There was confirmation that Bob was no stranger. 'Everybody knows Bob.'

'A dab hand at givin' you the right measure and not a drop more.'

'A dab hand.'

'The other night there he was limpin' about like a fella with a wooden leg. He wasn't at himself, he said. Hurted his toe. He gave one fella the wrong order twice. A half pint of draught instead of one by the neck.'

'Imagine anybody doin' a thing like that.'

'The fella didn't like it. "Bob," he says to him. "Bob. Yir fut's gone to yer head so it has." It wasn't a word of a lie.'

'Once he fell over at the pictures. It was all them names.'

A glance along the dialect shelves of most bookshops or public libraries will reveal the existence of a number of primers claiming to enable you to teach yourself Geordie, Tyke, Scouse, or even Bristle.

Their authors more or less guarantee that with some study it is possible to speak these dialects almost as fluently as a native.

Textbooks devoted to the intricacies of Northern Ireland speech are a lot less common. The difficulty is that the Ulster vernacular follows no set rules. There are no conventions. Practically everything goes.

You are born with its distinctive style of expression or you are not. It is a gift that cannot be acquired through study.

A definitive guide would run into massive difficulties in explaining the why and wherefore of the Belfast speech patterns displayed in such examples as—

'What's he till yew?'

'Them wee girls is the boys these days.'

'Once he fell over at the pictures. It was all them names.'

'He's a fren.'

'Ach but the sea was boggin'.'

'At the end he was ony middlin'.'

'Ye cudden givvus the time?'

The first simply seeks to establish the relationship between the individual questioned and a third person.

The second assesses the boisterous qualities of today's teenage misses.

The third describes the husband who dozed off at the cinema during the showing of a long list of credits.

The fourth was the comment of a man in a bus as he indicated an acquaintance in another seat.

The fifth is a disgusted description of the polluted Mediterranean by a returning holidaymaker.

The sixth gives the words of a man describing the last days of a friend.

The seventh chooses to put the question directly to you in preference to dialling TIM.

Phrasing in Ulster flaunts disciplines. There is no recognition whatever of such requirements as past participles, gerunds, whether or not it is correct to use a singular noun before a plural subject. These are trivialities to be swept ruthlessly aside.

There are thus obvious problems in compiling an at-a-glance guide which would enable an alien to check on the spot such statements as

'He spiles her. He giv her a buncha flars.'

'Them dures — when they're openin' they're closin'.'

'The chile's a wee dote.'

'If yousins don't get up I'll knock ye down.'

In these examples reference is being made to a husband who bought his wife flowers for her birthday, to the revolving doors at a city store, and to a well-behaved youngster. The final quotation represents the warning to a group of children sitting on a narrow pavement, given by a woman pushing a pram.

Take the case of an English visitor in search of a shop near the Albert Memorial clock tower, a Belfast landmark.

'It's fornint the big clauk,' he was told.

'What?' he asked in bewilderment.

'It's fornint the big clauk.'

'What do you mean?' the baffled visitor demanded.

'IT'S FORNINT THE BIG CLAUK,' his informant roared loudly, so loudly now that a small crowd began to gather and the inquirer's confusion grew.

Yet again the bawling voice insisted 'IT'S FORNINT THE BIG CLAUK' when someone stepped in with a quick translation and the embarrassed visitor fled. He had learned his lesson.

A guide to the intricacies of Geordie makes the claim 'When a Geordie speaks on any subject it sounds like part of a Pontifical High Mass.'

This may be so but for my money the speech of Yorkshire is not without considerable hurdles for the uninitiated.

When it comes to the speech of Bristolians (they call it Bristle) one aspect is a tendency to run words together. There you will hear 'armchair', which means 'How much do they cost?' In Ulster 'Whaddyalukkin?' means 'How much are you asking?' In at least one respect there is something in common.

In respect of Scouse my experience confirms the charge I have heard, 'Liverpool people cannot rub as much as two sentences together without the sparks of four-letter words flying in the air.'

Ulster people can normally express themselves without going quite so far. As a rule it can be said that everyday speech is much less inflamed with four-letter expressions than is the case with other idioms. Possibly it reflects a superior vocabulary.

If there are any hidden ground rules about the manner in which the Queen's English is used in Ulster they certainly do not mean that people watch their language, however. The point is that the results justify the flexibility.

Matter-of-factness keeps popping up. A Belfastman, asked to name his favourite flower, said quite explicitly 'Oatmeal.'

Actually the desire to make the position crystal clear almost seems to be a passion in Ulster.

When asked if her husband is at home a woman will answer 'He's in but he's out,' which means he's working in the garden.

If he has gone to the corner for cigarettes she will reply, 'He's not away. It's just that he's not here.'

In seeking to point out that she herself has been busy in the garden she will explain 'Sure I've been out since I came in.'

Observe to her that her pet dog seems to be off form and she will reply 'It's no well at all alo the tail.'

A degree of local knowledge is needed to understand the implications of the statement 'I was tuk.'

This can indicate that the speaker was given a lift by a friend, was cheated, or was taken to a show by an acquaintance who paid for the tickets.

'He's away' can mean that the individual concerned has gone on holiday, has launched himself on a familiar hobby-horse, or begun an often-told story once again.

I have been told of the startling effect of an inquiry about a patient at a Belfast hospital. It has taught them to be careful what they say. The answer was given to a caller 'He has gone home.' The inquirer promptly fainted, although all that was meant was that the patient had been discharged.

Which shows that even local knowledge sometimes fails to be all-embracing.

One arena in which a guide could be provided without too much difficulty would be in relation to measurements. Ulster people appear to use standards of their own, not in any way related to metric.

It takes a close friend to appreciate what is meant when a guest for tea is asked 'Do you take milk?' and replies 'Just what would colour it.'

When a neighbour is asked 'Could you lend me a wee known of milk?' she knows at once how much is sought. It could well be that four knowns make one pint but there are no authoritative grounds for saying so. The point is that a nice sense of delicacy is implied.

It will be said of a spendthrift 'He hasn't a gleed', which is self-explanatory while 'There isn't a tent of water in the kettle' will be clearly understood even if the hearer has no idea just how much a 'tent' literally represents.

A woman buying a pair of shoes will explain why her choice was for something less expensive than those she was offered by 'These'll do me for wearin' behind the chile's pram.'

And someone making a modest purchase in a cake shop will cover up by remarking, 'It's ony if anybody would walk in on me.'

So, too, a nice sense of propriety is demonstrated by the experience of the visitor who was asked by her hostess as the evening wore on 'Are you sure you're comfortable?'

Thinking she was being consulted about the cosiness of her chair she kept insisting that she was quite happy. It was only when the question was repeated several times that it was realised that it was another way of asking 'Do you want to use the toilet?'

On less formal occasions the need to answer the call of nature is explicitly indicated by 'I hafta go till the classet' or 'I'm away to the rinal.'

All are part and parcel of the Ulster speech syndrome, as individual as the comment of the woman visiting a bereaved neighbour. She was seen to regard the corpse with a profound expression of sadness and then murmured, 'Ach but you have her quare an' comfortable lookin'.'

And if there was to be a rigid observance of the incongruous in our utterances it would be deplorable to be deprived of the reply given by a Co Down woman to an inquiry about her husband's health, 'He's doin' not so bad only he still has his chest.'

'Mantannie can be quaren cuttin'.'

The impression is constantly created in Ulster of the existence of a private language, filled with intimate allusions that seem to have been deliberately designed to keep the stranger guessing, to drive it home that he must make his own effort to understand.

In fact it is a challenge that will be found to be well worth accepting. The rewards for the outsider are considerable.

Continual reference will be made to 'the brother', to 'Muncle Sidney' or 'Mant Bella'. Once it is grasped who is meant it makes all the difference.

Cousins, brothers-in-law, mischievious nephews, 'far-out friends' are persistently quoted. It is assumed that because of the relationship what they have to say has an added interest. Once the listener is prepared to acknowledge this a new world is opened up.

'Take the bror now,' you will be told. 'He said he had to stay in the house because his corn was leppin'.' It is beyond question that 'the bror' has been transformed into a figure of interest. You want to hear more about the man.

There will be the explanation, 'Take Muncle James. A rare turn. Always wears a check duncher and loves a nyarly fry.' Curiosity is promptly aroused. Actually the dish consists of a well-fried egg, fried soda bread, potato bread, bacon and mushrooms. It represents the last word in a fry.

Aunt Annie is equally colourful. 'Mantannie knows the side her bread's buttered on. When it comes to the bit, she knows. People say she can be quaren cuttin' but I wudn't say a word agin her.'

No attempt is made to provide a build up of the relation for the stranger's benefit. If there is a misunderstanding it is solely the fault of the listener. You have been brought into the family circle. It is up to you to do the rest.

Within seconds of starting a conversation with a stranger the Ulsterman will plunge into references to the men and women who fill his world, confident that they are worth talking about.

'If there's anybody I can't stand it's Big Sammy. He's on the wife's side of the family. Got hit on the fut with a paver the orr day there. More's the pity, I said to myself, he wasn't stannin' on his head at the time.'

Ulster people clearly have a profound belief in the philosophy which says 'Welcome to my world.'

'Minnie, now. You'd like Minnie. But the fella she's goin' with. He's not right for her. Has a fut like a doorstep. A gaunch.'

'Take Big Alec. Married on my sister, Jinny. He heard about the way they were treatin' their wee lad at school. He foamed up the teacher and told him straight, "Catch yourself on, mister. Just catch yourself on."'

'It's well seen William James's Roberta landed on her feet. They say she's nivver wet her hands since she married Shuey.'

The words, 'It's well seen' have a wide following for introducing a comment.

'It's well seen Muncle Seamus has a good memory for forgettin'.'

'It's well seen Big Aggie knows what side her bread's buttered on.'

An utter stranger will be greeted with the words, 'How's the boy?' His best bet is to treat it in the same style as the more conventional Ulster greeting, 'How's about ye?'

Another usage apt to confuse those unaccustomed to it is 'My hand on your new suit.' It could also be 'My hand on your shoes' or 'My hand on your coat.' This is intended to convey that what you are wearing has been noticed, maybe envied if it is unusual, although faint derision can also be implied.

Between close friends it can mean, 'That's not your usual style, is it?'

It is yet another usage guaranteed to cause the foreigner to stumble, like the message on a postcard sent to me from Benidorm. The writer quoted a snatch of conversation she overheard from the next table in a cafe. The Northern Ireland accent was quite marked.

'Take about prunes,' it ran. 'Them figs is the quare mark.'

I am convinced that no one could have understood what exactly was meant until the card reached Ulster.

'We didn't half go coming back,' is another sample of the vernacular that calls for local knowledge. It indicates that the return journey was made with all haste.

'I have every Saturday about off' similarly illustrates what would appear to be a private language. The message is, in fact, 'I'm off every alternative Saturday.'

'I'll take a wee skite over' has no implications of an intention to drop in, bearing whatever 'a wee skite' might be. The plan is simply to call for a short chat.

'It's all Annie Morgan' is used in some country districts to imply 'Everything you say is untrue.' Actually the lady is only one of many personalities who have found their way into the vocabulary.

A workman will say, 'I've been as busy as Baxter.'

The comment will be made, 'You're as far away as Kitty Logue.'

Anyone who behaves extravagantly will be referred to as 'Posy Cobain'.

'The wee Falorey man' can cover any regular caller of small stature. It can

'Keep an eye on the corner in case they've decided to walk home.'

be used to refer to the postman as readily as the milkman.

A common Ulster variant of 'a right Charlie' is 'He's a right oul Archie'.

'They were goin' along arm in arm like Betty Patterson,' indicates a blossoming romance.

'Katy Ann' is often used to indicate stress and could possibly by rhyming slang for 'damn'. For a really disastrous happening it can become 'Katy Ann Magee'.

They all serve to emphasise how much Ulster uses a shorthand of its own just as much as Yorkshire or Newcastle.

In a Belfast supermarket queue I heard this item of family history which would create obvious problems if it had to be translated for the benefit of an alien:

'The bror's a right slabber. If ever there was a right oul Archie it's our Patrick James. Fella that lives next door till him is a great boy for the pigeons. Last week there he was out searchin' the skies for his birds. They were due home from a race but there was neither hilt nor hare of them. So what d'ye think the bror says till him? "Keep an eye on the corner when you're at it," he says, "in case they've decided to walk home."'

'Could I see some of your soft men's hats?'

Supermarkets have made formidable inroads on the shop at the corner and its role in the Ulster way of life. Nevertheless over-the-counter shopping lingers still, and the homely philosophy for which it has long been a sounding board continues to echo amidst the stocks of butter and bacon, the shirts and the ties, the shoes and the hardware.

Visit one of the Province's 'wee shops' that doggedly defy the march of time, listen, and it is instantly obvious that it would be madness to start up a retail business in Ulster without a sound knowledge of the language of the people.

Trouble is ahead, for example, if there is not instant awareness of what is wanted by the request 'Can I have half a pound of navy blue grapes,' or 'Could I see your soft men's hats?'

Customers can turn awkward if they are made to look obtuse. Tact is important if a sale is to be made.

'Have you any revulsion paint?' was one order.

'Do you have a pair of boy's trousers to fit a man?'

'Revulsion? Don't you mean emulsion paint?' the customer was asked.

'I mean what I say, mister', was the sharp response, 'and if you haven't got any I can go elsewhere for it.'

Suggest that she should 'go ahead' and you have lost a customer for life.

Not everywhere would there be immediate understanding of what was in mind when a woman produced a left-hand glove and asked, 'Would you have a morrow for this?'

The successful trader must be for ever on his toes, never put out, no matter what might be the request.

'Would you have a pair of boy's trousers to fit a man?'

'Are your toilet rolls non-skid?'

'I'm looking a pair of trouser clips for a bicycle.'

A shop visit is usually considered an excuse for a chat. The specific purchase is invariably incidental.

'Do you know this? What's not up is rising, so it is.'

'I've run in for half a pound of butter in case I run out.'

'This is the second time I've been in here this morning. When I came last time he hadn't his ribs in.'

Often the shop-counter is a kind of confessional.

'My man's wore the same suit for forty years and if God spares him he'll wear it till he goes.'

'I'm going to have to buy the wee lad another pair of them demins. The ones I bought him a wee while ago — I might as well not bothered. He had the arse out of the knee of them before you could blink your eyes.'

'I bought a pound of steak last week and the jaws of hell wouldn't eat it.'

'I'll have to fly. The potatoes are peeled but I have to put a match to them.'

Puzzling moments for the uninitiated are inevitable. This was the case with the visitor who was left wondering what treat could be ahead when, in a crowded establishment, a stranger who wanted past said to him, 'Would you mind letting me by you?'

He was no less bewildered as he was leaving. A heavily laden woman had the door opened for her by a helpful new arrival who said, 'I see you have no hands.'

It is vital that the shopkeeper should be able to hold his own at all times.

'Do you sell corn plasters?' one was asked.

'How many do you want?'

'Howl on just a wee minute.' The customer began adding up on his fingers. 'One on every toe and three on the sole of my right fut. That makes eight. Then the five on the sole of my other fut. That's thirteen.'

'Man, but you have a right crop,' was the reply. 'You're lucky you have only two feet or you'd have needed one of them combined harvesters.'

A different note was struck by the man who said he wanted 'One pence worth of insect powder.'

'One pence worth,' came the protest. 'Man dear, that wouldn't pay for the paper and the time and trouble of wrapping it up.'

'Who said anything about wrapping it up. I just want you to dust it down my back.'

A country shopkeeper was asked if she sold tacks, replied that she had them in stock, discovered she was wrong, and beamingly told the customer 'Fancy me saying me has tacks and me has no tacks.'

Firmness is needed when the patronage is juvenile. One small boy's order was for 'A pence worth of them mixed caramels.'

'Here's two,' the shopkeeper told him. 'Mix them yourself.'

Shoe shops are a particularly fruitful source of colourful comment.

'These oul shoes is crucifyin' me,' moaned a woman in one of them. A companion in similar agony was heard to say, 'It's terrible. Sure my left-hand fut is drainin' the life's blood outa me.'

Assistants inevitably become hardened to the lamentations of their customers. They will usually take it in their stride when the request runs, 'I want a pair of sensible shoes for wearing,' and tactfully refrain from asking, 'Do you usually buy them for throwing at people?'

One shopper blandly announced, 'I want a pair with plenty of room in them. I got a bad fut from the last pair I bought and it stuck out like a sore thumb.'

A woman who had selected a pair after a lengthy process of trial said, 'These ones are just right. They fit me like a glove.' It is the kind of verdict that helps to make the sorely tried assistant's day.

In Ulster the importance of being well shod is driven home from an early age. This was shown by the admonition of the parent who had just bought his small son a new pair of soes.

They were setting out to visit relations and the boy said proudly, 'Da, I've got my new shoes on.'

'That's all right then,' the father said, 'but be sure to take bigger strides.'

In another footwear store a woman complained, 'Between blisters and bunions I haven't a fut to walk on. Cud ye do somethin' for me?'

An ability to handle all kinds of requests with aplomb is needed behind the counter. A general store where practically everything is stocked was the scene of an encounter involving a man who wanted to buy 'a china dog for the mantelpiece'.

'We have a wide selection,' he was told. 'Do you want a pair?'

'No, not a pair, Just one. I have a pair but one of them got broken.'

'It'll be no trouble to replace it,' he was assured. 'Is it a right hand dog or a left hand one you want?'

The customer thought for a moment, then said, 'Dammit but I couldn't rightly say. All I can tell you is that its backside points straight down the main street of Stewartstown.'

'There was the smell of death off her.'

To overhear the comment 'He's very like himself' by no means infers that the speaker is, perhaps, studying a friend's photograph. The reality is that she is looking at his corpse.

The words are intended to be complimentary; not that the deceased could have had the misfortune to look like his wife.

The remarks inspired by a bereavement cover an extensive litany. They can be a constant source of surprise to the stranger.

The statement, 'If he'd been living he'd have been a month dead this Saturday' may sound complicated but this is not the intention. The motivation is a desire to show that there has been a careful and precise reckoning of the passage of time since the bereavement.

A person can 'die of a Thursday' just as readily as 'of a heart attack'.

Reactions to the news of someone's demise can have unexpected forms.

'My uncle. He's dead so he is.'

'When did it happen?'

'Only yesterday.'

'Away to hell.'

It is important to appreciate that the comment really means, 'You don't say!' or 'I just can't believe it.'

Praising the virtues of the deceased in verse in the obituary columns of the newspapers is a custom now rarely observed. Formerly it was common for a death notice to be accompanied by such lines as

> *On earth she toiled.*
> *In heaven she rests.*
> *God bless you Trisha*
> *You were one of the best.*

Another example of poetic effort that somehow did not quite come off ran

> *Where she has gone we do not know.*
> *We cannot tell her of our woe.*
> *Tell how we miss our dearest Tess.*
> *She's gone, alas, and left no address.*

Exchanges to be heard in the home of the deceased can take unusual forms.

'I'm awful sorry. What killed him?'

'I haven't actually heard but it musta been something serious.'

'Yes, ye cud be right. It said sudden in the paper.'

One unexpected reaction came from a man who had already heard the news from several sources, 'Sure he's dead already.'

A woman, beholding the remains of a neighbour, summed up the sad situation with the words, 'Ach isn't it well for her. There she is with her head all happed up in glory and here we are and God knows what's going to happen to us.'

A passing custom was to have the deceased laid out by women who earned a small fee for the service.

A 'layer out' had been told that there had been a request that the dead woman should be garbed in the navy costume she constantly wore. This was duly done but the 'dresser' indicated some dissatisfaction with the result.

'Somehow she doesn't look right,' she complained. 'Something's missing. I can't think what it is.'

'I know,' said one of the bereaved relations. 'It's her black umbrella. She never went anywhere without her black umbrella.'

The umbrella was duly placed beside the coffin and all was well.

When undertakers talk 'shop' in Ulster the pattern is little different to that anywhere else.

Two members of the profession met in the street and one mentioned that a well known resident had died and wondered who had carried out the funeral arrangements.

When the name of a third undertaker was mentioned the comment immediately came, 'He didn't! Dammit if he had been alive we'd have done it.'

People gravely ill and not expected to recover are the cause of unexpected pronouncements.

'Last time I saw the soul I knew there was the smell of death off her.'

'I was sure he wasn't going to do.'

'I just knew the gravedigger had shook his shovel at her. I knew it in my bones.'

In most cases compliments to the character of the deceased come thick and fast, however undeserved. There can, however, be exceptions.

A couple travelling home from a funeral saw a member of the family, stopped the car, and called to him.

'Hello Uncle James,' one greeted him. 'We're just coming back after burying Aunt Martha. Hadn't you heard about her?'

'No I hadn't,' the reply came, 'but I hope you put your foot on her and saw she was well down.'

A death in the family can sometimes have quite unpredictable effects.

This request was made in a Belfast post office, 'Cudda have a stamp of a nice quiet colour? It's for a letter of sympathy to a friend with a dead niece.'

No less unexpected was the call made on the owner of a hardware shop. A woman said she wanted a 'wee wooden box'.

He produced several boxes, all without success, and finally asked 'Tell me, missus. What exactly is the box for?'

'It's for Samuel James,' was the admission. 'I want it to prop up the head of his coffin so that his friends can get a better look at him.'

A conversation at the obsequies of a woman noted for her compulsive neatness about the house took its inevitable turn.

'Sure she never rested; never stopped tidying up the house.'

'Know what I'm going to tell you? When the hearse is taking her to the graveyard she'll likely get up to see if the coffin handles are shining enough to please her.'

'Aye, and if they don't she'll haugh on them and use her shroud to shine them up.'

Sympathy can take unusual forms. A tribute of a kind was intended when a visitor who called on a bereaved family gave the corpse a long, sad appraisal, spoke of the fact that the man had died after a stay at the seaside, and murmured, 'Ach but you can see the holiday did him a world of good.'

'My man's over on his knees eating crumpets.'

It would be difficult to give an authoritative answer to the question, 'Who makes the biggest contribution to colourful Ulster speech? Men or women?'

As the preceding chapters show, the ladies are responsible for a not inconsiderable contribution. The examples that keep coming my way emphasise that if the women of the Province were to be struck dumb en masse the loss in sparkling language would be much more than fifty per cent.

The troubled years of recent history have produced their own feminine interpretation of their impact on everyday existence. Housewives may not have been the most prominent protagonists in the violence, although they have not stood aside from it, but they have their own attitude to it all.

This is typified by the woman in one of the borderline areas of Belfast, where knee-capping had become a fact of life.

A small boy, interested in her fox terrier, asked her, 'Missus, wud that wee dog of yours bite?'

'Bite? Child dear, it won't even bark. On top of that it's a soldier lover, so it is. It licks their hands, wags its tail, and follows them. One of these days it'll be the instigation of me getting knee-capped so it will.'

No pet could have been more caustically indicted.

In the same field of endeavour was the woman with a neighbour who had taken full advantage of a bomb attack on a furniture shop in the district and had acquired a quantity of 'souvenirs' of the occasion.

'Did she get much?' the question was asked.

'For God's sake, you should have seen her house,' was the awed answer. 'She had that much carpet on the flure you would have thought you were walkin' on horse manure.'

There is a flavour of its own about the complaint heard in another battered area of Belfast, 'Maggie dear, you have no conception of how bad it was. I hadda have the windas boarded up with lumps of tin.'

Matters were neatly summarised in the comment inspired by the removal of security barricades in a town centre, 'Know what I'm goin' till tell ye? Since they tuk away the barricades the mudguards wud take the behind aff ye.'

The woman who told a friend 'I got my windas done' could have meant (a) the window cleaner has been, (b) they have been newly painted, or (c) they have been broken as a result of stone throwing. The odds would usually

'That dog's a soldier lover, so it is.'

favour (c).

The wife of the owner of a shop badly damaged by incendiaries was heard to say, her voice filled with wonder, 'There was none of it left standing except the basement. You could hardly credit it.'

Two women in a bus were discussing clashes that had followed band parades in the district.

'What d'ye think of the carry-on last night?' one inquired. 'Wasn't it a terrible business?'

'D'ye know this?' came the reply, the tone highly confidential. 'I'm now seventy-five. My father was a Presbyterian and my man's a Roman Catholic. I just don't take any part in these things because at my time of life I'm anxious not to fall out either with the dead or the livin'.'

Women tend to lift the lid on family skeletons to a greater degree than husbands.

Complete strangers will be told, 'When my man was alive he was a great believer in porridge for his bowels.'

'D'ye know this? My husband never had a bad back till the day they buried him.'

It's a quare funny thing. My man's over on his knees eatin' crumpets.'

'Take my husband now. Joseph. He doesn't like coffee because he says it doesn't taste like tea.'

The intimate personal details, made known with such readiness, certainly enable the hearer to picture the individual referred to much more easily than a wordy physical description.

The revelations are not confined to husbands.

'There's the brother. He's a one. Last week there he saw the doctor and told him his bowels moved like clockwork every mornin' at seven. What's the trouble then, the doctor ast. "Sure the trouble is," the brother said, "I never waken till eight so I don't."'

Rather different qualities were to be encountered in another speaker's Uncle Albert, a man obviously interested in music — the more martial the better.

'He's a terbil man for a bit of a tune.'

'What kind of a band does he play in then?'

'I couldn't rightly say what kind. All I know is that it's not a brass band. It's one of them slitter slatter ones.'

Praise can come as readily as criticism.

'My sister's wee lad is a great wee character. Never late for school, always neat and tidy, always gets his sums right. As for his writing a blind man could read it.'

'Aye, but is he good natured with it all?'

'Good natured? Sure the wee cratur would ate potato skins.'

The other side of the coin was being discussed in a different case.

'I bought our wee Desmond a school blazer and he just won't wear it so he won't. I don't know what's got into him. If I hadn't got it for him it would never be off his back.'

Parental tribulations appear to be never-ending.

'I told the wee bugger right out. When I get you in, I said, may the Lord have mercy on your behind.'

Clothes give the family a close run as a subject for comment.

'That lovely new coat. I was that fond of it. It was stole?'

'I didn't know you had a fur coat.'

'Ach, woman dear. It was stole, I mean. Somebody broke into the house one night we were out. They tuk it an' my man's transistor. But it wus losin' the coat that just broke my heart. Not one of the neighbours saw it on me. Imagine.'

Ulsterwomen can bring a sense of wonder to their pronouncements that often gives them an extra dimension.

'Dierdre's morr was round till see me. I told her I didn't hear her knock the first time and she gave me a quare funny look.'

'You don't meet many like big Kevin. I wudn't call him educated, mind ye. All he wants is a plateful of dip and he's as happy as Larry.'

'William James, he has a heart of gold but when he takes the notion he has a quare brass neck.'

In similar strain was the complaint made about a pushing new shopkeeper by one of his customers, 'He ast me if I wud like a nice chandelier. Cheap, he said. Imagine! A chandelier! And not one in our house knows a note of music.'

To a lesser extent in modern times than was once the case the main requirement of a farmer's wife was to be 'well wrought'.

This led to the comment about one firm Co. Antrim bachelor, 'Any woman Wullie wud take for a wife wud need to be wrought specially for him in a foundry, so she would.'

No less down to earth was the verdict delivered by one young woman to her companion, 'Sure the oul maids have the best of it — if it wasnae for the disgrace.'

Surprisingly, the stranger who asks the way in Ulster will find it much more informative to ask a man rather than a woman. Women tend to be embarrassed when accosted by someone they don't know.

It was a man who gave this piece of advice, 'To get there go on up that lane and turn down a wee street you'll see in front of you. It's at the other end of it. I don't know if it's there now or not, mind you. It was there anyway when I was a wee lad.'

Another local guide put his directions like this, 'Drive on till you see a wee pub with a tan roof and you'll find you aren't a hare's lep from the place.'

Even more specific was the counsel, 'Walk on till you come to the next burn and you're at it,' although running it close was the instruction, 'Go straight down the road and it's on the left after the second bump on the road.'

'There's more of me in thon hospital than there is in me.'

It is difficult not to have a spark of sympathy for the Ulsterman who had been to see his doctor and later lamented, 'I might as well not have went for I'm home with a bottle for my stummick and it was a bad head I went to him with.'

Complications involving the state of one's health tend to become unusually involved in Ulster. Nothing ever seems to be completely straightforward.

A case in point is provided by the lady of whom it was said, 'She's on her back again with her bad leg.'

And this dialogue in a chemist's would have a lot of people wondering what it was all about.

A woman having a prescription made up was asked, 'Will you take it now or would you rather come back for it?'

'I'll not bother now. I'll just take it when I get home.'

Revelations in the surgery can take the most unexpected forms.

'Sure he's that wake if he'd been shot through the heart he'd of had to be helped to the flure.'

'The wee lad's streamin' with the cowl. He was stannin' in the jam of the dure without a bite in his stummick and his wee gensie was ringin', and him without a shoe to his fut.'

A cry from the heart would seem to be an apt description of the lament of one woman, 'There're more of me in thon hospital than there is in me and they want me back in three months to see if there's anything else they can lay their hands on.'

In many cases going to see the doctor is considered a last resort. 'Missus

McClatchey, would you have a look at this boil of mine, like a good woman. If it wasn't where it is I'd ask the doctor to give me a jeg.'

GPs have to be long-suffering mortals. Those who are not are unlikely to survive.

One of them asked a patient, 'Have you been to any doctor before coming to me?'

'No,' came the reply. 'I went to the chemist.'

'The chemist? And what stupid advice did you get from him?'

'He told me to come and see you.'

Another was asked by a patient's wife what he really thought of him.

'To tell you the truth,' he said candidly, 'I don't think I like the look of him.'

'Neither do I, doctor, but he's awful good to the children.'

A woman outlined her complaint and her success in getting over it by saying, 'I had a wee touch of killitis. I thought it was going to be the end of me but I sheughed if off and now I'm as right as rain. Nearly, anyway.'

A patient who had managed to reach a considerable age was asked to what he felt he owed his longevity.

'Ninety-two years is a fair stretch,' he was told. 'Did you always look after yourself?'

'No more than the next fella,' was the answer. 'It's the weather. That's what did it. It's terrible in this part of the world.'

'But what has the weather to do with it?' came the query.

'Ach sure, it puts years on you.'

Conversations in the doctor's waiting room are invariably intimate, as well as revealing.

'Have ye a dose?' a woman asked the occupant of the next seat.

'A'm full of it. If A had cum full sprachle on a load a stanes I cudna feel worse.'

'Be the sound of ye ye're fit for yir bed.'

'Me? Woman dear a'm fit for nathin'.'

The waiting room was full and the doctor was late. Everyone fidgeted impatiently until finally one of the frustrated patients was heard to exclaim, 'It isn't good enough. He must think we're here for the good of our health.'

It is probable that in no other part of the British Isles would there be heard a reply anything akin to that uttered by a man who had been given a bottle and was asked how he was. 'It's like this. I'm better now than I was before but not as well as I was before I was as bad as I am now.'

One woman in a state of some anxiety about her husband's health decided to consult a neighbour and asked her, 'Tell me this and tell me no more, Denise. Does your man ever talk to himself?'

'Sure how would I know whether he does or not? I'm never with him when he's by himself.'

'I'd like an ever-ready turkey.'

Imprecise use of words is no more exclusive to one area of the country than another. Certainly the tendency to make a stagger at it if the exact word just cannot be recalled has gone a long way since Mrs Malaprop.

It could be said to have gone no further than in Ulster, which has made its own firm contribution to the trend.

Shopkeepers especially are the targets for the penchant of clawing the air for the wanted word and grasping at one that *sounds* like it. It produces requests like:

'Would you give me a cartoon of milk?'

'I want some of that mental snuff.'

'I'd like an ever-ready turkey.'

'Have you any cannibal's soup?'

'I'm lookin' for some blattered fish fingers.'

'Could I have half-a-dozen mandoline oranges?'

'Givvus half a pound of dislocated coconut.' (Occasionally this will be varied to 'constipated coconut'.)

A woman describing an accident to her husband added the graphic detail, 'A cartridge shot out of his leg.'

She had the same word power as the tenant who complained to her rent collector, 'You'll hafta do something about the condescension on the windows. It's driving me up the walls.'

'Sympathise your watches' was the order given to a hiking party about to set off in the Mournes.

Understanding was not so swift at the chemist's where a woman asked, 'Could I have a tube of dorodent?'

When she was handed a tube of Mum she looked at it in disgust and protested, 'What good is that? Sure that wouldn't get rid of those rats we have.'

Health is a frequent inspiration for Malapropisms.

'I'm going to ask the doctor for a description.'

'I'm suffering from general ability.'

'The child was up all night with abominable pains.'

'I'm going to see one of them soroptimists about my feet.'

An accolade of sorts is surely earned by the holidaymaker on the Continent who said, 'We all went up on a vernacular railway.'

The statement has an affinity of sorts to that of the woman who spoke of the 'Royal Ulster Vocabulary'.

Another holiday example alluded to the bather who was 'swept to sea on a lido', and there was a tourist who paid this tribute to her hotel, 'The spring inferior mattresses were powerful.'

I have been told of the woman who insisted, 'When he heard, the oul fella jumped up and down with incitement,' and went on to refer to the man who 'went down like a bursted baboon'.

Said to have been overheard in a black taxi was the revelation, 'Our Martha never misses the horoscopes. I'm a Virgo but she's an Episcopalian.'

This emphasises that religous beliefs do not escape. The woman who told a friend, 'I had a couple of Normans on the doorstep yesterday,' had an understanding companion who said, 'Aye, and we had one of them Seven Day Adventurers.'

It is some years since I was first told of the Belfastman who was asked, 'You don't happen to be a Jehovah's Witness, do you?' and answered, 'Why, has there been an accident?' I have since noticed that Bob Hope has also heard of him.

The impulse to be the bearer of good tidings constantly inspires the ludicrous:

'There's a cousin I have in Scotland. He's doing awful well. He's just been made a county survivor.'

'There's one thing about Sally's man. He's always miraculously dressed.' I fancy the spreaker would get on well with the woman who insisted, 'To my mind it's a matter of pure congestion.'

Not every shopper would appreciate the advice a woman was given in a large store when she sought the way to another department, 'It's on the next floor up but sure you could go by the excavator there and save time.'

The insistence on the word that isn't quite right never seems to stop.

'I'm thinking of getting myself a pair of them contract lenses.'

'You should hear my husband. He says he's going to stop getting the Sunday papers. What he doesn't like about them is that they're full of sex mechanics.'

'The wee lad did his level best but he lost that many points he was illuminated.'

'At the match on Saturday our Brendan was sent to the civilian.'

'They were in Rome for their holidays and saw the Cistern Chapel at the Vatican.'

'I had to take the cat to the vet to get it bluthered.'

'They went out in the yard and assaulted themselves.'

'Our milk was paralysed by a Government anarchist.'

The Province's violent years have produced their quota of misplaced expressions.

'When it comes to stoppin' the cowboys with the guns there's no better detergent than a policeman on the beat.'

'The cause of half the trouble is italiation, so it is.'

'With all these troubles you need an apprehensive policy on your house.'

'All this shootin' an' murderin' — what good is beyond my condecension.'

'I got three sanitary bombs through the window.'

Beyond question, the ghost of Mrs Malaprop haunts Belfast, and does so energetically. What better evidence than the woman who was explaining to a friend that she planned to have her kitchen tiled?

'I ast these two men to give me an estimate so they poked all round it, then they went out into the yard and assaulted themselves, and came back and said it would be £10.'

The same lady turned out to be a mind of domestic chit chat:

'My sister has the electric but I have the gas. The only electric I use is one of them emergency heaters.'

'The wee lad got hurt last week,' she went on. 'He was a pavilion passenger on another fella's motor bike and it skid. And d'ye know what was wrong? The fella didn't have an adviser on his helmet.'

She spotted a neighbour who had been celebrating unwisely and was obviously having difficulty in finding his house. Helpfully she led him to his front door and told him, 'There you are, Bertie, You have reached your destiny.'

As she left him a deep sigh escaped her as she murmured, 'It's changed days. Sure, when Cathy married you she used to say you were an awful funny fella for you kept her in suspenders.'

'D'ye want me to draw my hand across yir gub?'

Just as it is possible to find a Yorkshireman (to say nothing of a Geordie) who will insist that their idiom can sometimes jar, so the speech of Northern Ireland has its critics.

These will include parents who prefer their children to be 'well spoken', for example, besides teachers of English, and pedants.

The side you are on depends on whether you believe in rebuking a troublesome child with a restrained, 'Would you please try and behave?' or favour roaring at them, 'D'ye want me to draw my hand across yir gub?'

Take a doorstep conversation between two talkative Belfastwomen, Aggie and Bella. They are old friends. They are standing chatting at Aggie's front door, their arms folded. They are women with all the time in the world.

AGGIE: Ach, howerye Bella? It's nice to get a breath av air. I'm awful warm for I'm just aff the griddle.[1]

BELLA: Right enough. It takes it outa ye.

AGGIE: See me? I don't mind the bakin' one bit. Made the wee lad a perr of trousers outa an oul perr of his da's and d'ye know, ye cudn't tell wherr he wiz comin' or goin'. I wuz nivver any use with a needle.

BELLA: Me nire. I cudn't make my wee Darathy a frack if ye wir to give me a medal. Headstrong wee article, mind ye. Wud drive ye up the walls.[2]

AGGIE: Don't talk. I tole my wee lad if he didn't catch hisself on I'd give him a right skelp and what d'ye think he said? Said he go an' tell the battered babies people on me, so he did.

BELLA: It makes ye think.

AGGIE: Ach, ye cudn't tell him aught. I nearly give him the rounds of the kitchen.[3]

BELLA: An' for why didden ye?

AGGIE: I toul him I'd tell his da. He'll murder ye, I toul him.

BELLA: That wud put him in his place.

AGGIE: Damn the put. The da has it in fer him anyway. He'll not miss him and hit the wall once he gets started.

BELLA: Childer! They're a handful.

AGGIE: Don't talk to me. Last week I found the wee whelp starin' inta the mare his da shaves in.[4] I ast him what he was doin'. 'Ye told me to watch myself, didden ye?' he says.

BELLA: There ye are ni.

AGGIE: Know what I m goin' till tell ye? I usta think it wud be that nice if he was the kind of wee lad that wud chase butterflies. No fear. All he'll ivver chase after is an oul ball. [5]

BELLA: Weans! All the same they can be the quare oul help when they like.

AGGIE: All the help they can be is to help ye spend yir money.

BELLA: It's no use talkin'.

AGGIE: Funny enough I was in the shap the orr day there and a woman beside me tole me she was havin' her sister's two wee girls for supper. Ye shudda seen the luck she got from the strange woman stannin' beside her. Honest to Gawd I believe the poor woman thought she was among a lock of cannibals.

BELLA: It makes ye think.

AGGIE: Then lo and behold the next mint wee Mrs Bickerstaff comes runnin' in an' says, 'I can't light the fire with the childer. Give me a coupla firelighters.' I thought the woman was goin' till claps. [6]

BELLA: My bror shudda been there. He was geggin' me for sayin' I'd got my ear back after I got it syringed. 'Who'd ye len' it to,' he asts.

AGGIE: Some people would make ye sick.

BELLA: Ach there's worse nor him. He's a brave sowl. [7] He tuk a photo of Alice an' her wee girl. An' d'ye know? I cudn't help thinkin' to myself, 'That wee infant's that like her morr it wud scare ye.'

AGGIE: It's like wee Willie John up the street. I remember thinkin' onct he'd be terrible like his morr if he didn't luck so much like his farr.

BELLA: Did ye hear about his morr? She's gat herself one of them tumbler dryers, I was towl.

AGGIE: Her? In Gawd's name what does she want with a tumbler dryer? Her morr nivver had one. Her morr always used mugs an' beakers and just renched them out in the jawbox. [8]

BELLA: Right enough she always wuz a bit av a put on. Her man's no different. Hasta have a blue plastick bax for his piece. [9] Brown paper isn't good enough.

AGGIE: A piece of the paper wud do the same boy rightly.

BELLA: Men!

AGGIE: See our Alfy? Nivver takes butter an' jam together. He likes them both right enough but not mixed.

BELLA: There's no pleasin' some of them. I ast the beefman for some stuin' mate for our Harry's tea and all he give me was a hirstle av bones. [10]

AGGIE: Alfy catched a wee bit of a cowl the orr day there and coughed all night.

BELLA: One thing about arwuns. Thanks be to Gawd they're all on their feet. [11]

AGGIE: Talkin' about feet, d'ye like my new glasses? Sure ye nivver said.

BELLA: Ach Aggie dear it wuz on the tip av my tongue so it wuz. They're lovely. They fairly furnish yir face.

AGGIE: The speck man toul me they were a great improvement and I ast him did he think I needed improvin'.

BELLA: Shopmen nowadays! They have the quare nerve. Last Friday was a fortnight I lucked at a sideboard in Richardson's but I didden take it tho. It was too long in the length.[12] The fella in the shap wuz all offended. For why shud I have bought it if it wasn't right?

AGGIE: Oul Richardson's a case. Ivvery time I see him I think that owl cap he wears lucks like a lightin' pad for pigeons.

BELLA: Ye cudn't be up till some of them.

AGGIE: He's not a patch on Jimmy in the hardware shap. I wuz in it luckin' for a shammy for the one I had wuz in ribbins.[13] A fella comes in wantin' a shovel. Jimmy points till a lock of them stannin' in a corner an' says 'Take yir pick.' 'It's a shovel I want,' the man says. 'Not a pick.'

BELLA: Jimmy! D'ye know his wife?

AGGIE: Her! I'd far rarr keep her a week than a fortnight. A trencher-woman if ivver there wuz one. As soon as the mate's set down till her she charges in with both feet in the trough.

BELLA: Ye cud take yir dead end at people like that.[14]

AGGIE: Know what I'm goin' till tell ye? I tuk my dead end at Archie an' his caravan down in Millisle. I wudn't go back till it if he got down on his knees. Sadie's weans were down and I tuk them a walk over the sand-hills. It pelted on me. The rain didn't take time till come down. I was destroyed before I got back. I wuz as stiff as a ten fut plank for a week.

BELLA: Give me a house with a front door any day.

AGGIE: It's the Gawd's truth. There's arr Eileen. She's in one av them new estates an' I ast her what they were like. She said it was all right but there wuz one thing she cudn't get used till. It's the yard, she says. It's up-stairs.[15]

BELLA: That kind of thing takes a bit av gettin' used till. It's like me the orr day. Threw out arr new teapot and didn't know there wur a coupla cups in it.[16] But I'll havta run. Stewart'll be home for his tay.

AGGIE: It was nice havin' a bit av yir crack but ye cud have been sittin' while ye were standin'.

BELLA: Sure nobody' has a mint nowadays.

AGGIE: So long, then. Tell Stewart I was astin about him.

BELLA: So I will. If I don't see you before next Tuesday I'll see ye after.

From the conversation the following can be established:

1 Aggie has just finished baking soda bread.
2 Bella finds her daughter Dorothy very trying.
3 Aggie has threatened to chastise her small son physically.
4 She has found him staring at himself in his father's shaving mirror.
5 He is clearly fond of playing football.
6 Aggie thought the woman near her was about to collapse.
7 Bella's brother is not a bad sort.
8 Willie John's mother always rinsed her mugs and beakers in the sink.
9 Her husband likes his packed lunch to be in a plastic box.
10 Bella asked her butcher for stewing meat and was given mainly bones.
11 Her family are in good shape. No one is laid up.
12 The sideboard was too long for the room.
13 Aggie's chamois needed replacement.
14 Bella is surprised at the way others behave.
15 Eileen finds it difficult to get used to an upstairs toilet.
16 Bella rinsed out the teapot, unaware that it wasn't quite empty.

'Amferaff' till 'Yilhafta'

This at-a-glance guide to the complications of Ulster speech embodies many of the words used in the preceding pages. It is designed to act as a tough decoder for the uninitated, to help them through the thickets of the every-day language of the people. It might even make life a shade easier for any Martian who might one day land in the Province.

AMFERAFF	I'm leaving.
ARMAY	My daughter, May. Can also refer to a sister or any other member of the family; e.g. 'Armay's a quare wee girl.'
ARRWUNS	Our family.
ANNAHYDION	Person ignorant by their own choice.
BAP	Head; e.g. 'Mind yir bap.' Swollen; e.g. 'It went up like a bap.' Dinner roll.
BAXER	Professional pugilist.
BETOBE	Inevitable; unavoidable.
BINLID	Irresponsible person; e.g. 'He's a stupit ijit. He was always a right binlid.'
BIRL	Dance; e.g. 'Wud ye like a wee birl?'
BLUTERED	Intoxicated.
BOXTY	Dish made of grated potatoes with a little flour and water added, then fried.
BOKE	Vomit; e.g. 'He was sick to the stummick. He started to boke all over the place.'
BUMSKERR	Bomb scare.
BUNALSKRAP	Valueless; second-hand car that fails to live up to expectations; e.g. 'This thing's a bunalskrap.'
CHAPS	Popular delicacy served with fish; salt and vinegar being added to taste. Often dished up in newspaper.

COGGLEY	Unsteady.
CORFORUS	Call for me; e.g. 'Corforus at eight.'
DIVID	Divide.
DOKE	Doagh, Co. Antrim village.
DOWER	Door, portal; e.g. 'He came in through the dower.'
DREITCH	Tedious.
DRIBBLE	Small amount; display clever footwork at soccer.
DROOKET	Wet through.
DRUTH	Someone fond of the bottle.
DUNCH	Sharp blow with the elbow or shoulder.
FAILED	In poor health; e.g. 'She's away to scrapens. When I saw her she was all failed.'
FEEL	Venue for Orange demonstration; place to sow crop of potatoes, corn, or wheat; e.g. 'That's a great feel of potatoes.'
FERNUF	'What you say is reasonable.'
FISSICK	Cure; pick-me-up; e.g. 'I want a wee fissick for my stummick.'
FLANNIN	Face flannel; e.g. 'There's a flannin in the jawbox if you want to wash your face.'
FOAMED	Telephoned.
FONLY	If only; e.g. 'Fonly I hadda known I wudda went.'
GANTING	Yawning; e.g. 'He was ganting all through the sermon.'
GAUNCH	Awkward individual; ignoramus.
GEEK	Peep; e.g. 'I took a wee geek through the keyhole.'
GITTONYE	Get dressed.
GLAR	Sticky mud.
GOOSEGAB	Gooseberry.
GORB	Person who over-eats; e.g. 'There she was stuffin' herself like the wee gorb that she is.'
GREETIN	Crying; e.g. 'She was greetin her eyes out at the wedding.'
GULPIN	Brainless idiot.
HIRPLE	To limp; e.g. 'He went hirpling down the road.'
HIYEW	'I say'; 'Hi there.'

HURSTLE	Speak hoarsely; e.g. 'He was awful hard to make out for he had a wee hurstle.'
JAMEMBER	'Do you recall?' e.g. 'Jamember the horse trams?'
JUNDERED	Jostled.
LUMP	Growing child; e.g. 'She's a right wee lump.'
MALE	Breakfast, lunch, or tea. More often dinner; e.g. 'He's a great believer in four square males a day.'
MANGEY	Mean, ungenerous.
MANTANNY	My Aunt Annie; e.g. 'Mantanny wud never ask you if you had a mouth on you.'
MARR	Mirror.
MINT	Minute; e.g. 'The train goes in five mints.'
MOWER	Additional amount; e.g. 'He's always lookin' for mower.'
MUNCLE	My uncle; e.g. 'Muncle's a character.' (See Mantanny)
NEG	Article of food provided by hens; scold; e.g. 'She nivver gives her man a minute's peace. All she does is neg.'
NI	The present; e.g. 'Are you goin' ni?'
NIRE	Neither; e.g. 'I'm the same, I don't like her nire.'
NOCKITAFF	'Stop it.'
NYARLY FRY	Solid fry of sausages, potatoes, bacon, egg and soda bread.
ORCHIN	Small boy; e.g. 'He's a bad wee orchin.'
ORRDAY	The other day; recently.
ORRDOOR	The other day.
OUL	Aged; held in regard; e.g. 'I only bought this bit of an oul coat yesterday.' Also, 'You're an oul dear.'
PANADA	Type of bread pudding.
PIECE	Shipyardman's packed lunch.
PILE	Large amount; e.g. 'I have a pile of smoothin' to do.'
PLANE	Children amusing themselves; e.g. 'They were plane in the street.'
PLUES	Linfield football team, so called because of their blue jerseys; e.g. 'The wee Plues can fairly play.'

POTATO CLOCK	'About eight o'clock.'
QUILT	Tedious bore; undependable person.
R	The surname Orr.
REDD	Clear up, especially after a meal. Tidy a room.
ROUGHNESS	Plentitude.
RUBITCH	Rubbish; e.g. 'He did nothin' but talk rubitch.'
SARDY	Saturday
SCRINGE	Shudder; noise made by grinding the teeth together.
SCUFFED	Worn, soiled; e.g. 'He got his new suit all scuffed.'
SCUNDERED	Frustrated; bitterly disappointed.
SCUT	Poor type of person; e.g. 'He's nothing more than a drunken scut.'
SHAMMY	Chamois.
SKELPH	Splinter of wood; e.g. 'I got a skelph in my thumb.'
SKITTER	Low character (See Slabber).
SMITTLE	Infectious.
SPEELEY	Climb with agility; e.g. 'Watch me speeley up the lamp-post.'
SPUCKETING	It is raining heavily; e.g. 'We won't be able to go out. Spucketing.'
STEW	Is that you?
STRY	It has stopped raining; e.g. 'We can go out now, Stry.' (See Spucketing).
STOON	Throbbing pain.
SMEE	'It's me.'
TARGE	Ill-tempered, querulous woman.
TERL	Towel; e.g. 'He threw in the terl.'
TERBIL	Terrible, disastrous.
THASHES	Remnants of a fire; e.g. 'This shop has riz from thashes.'
THARCHES	Holywood Arches, Belfast landmark.
THERENI	Recently; expression of sympathy; e.g. 'Thereni, don't don't worry your head. Everything will be all right.'
TURNED	Gone sour, changed religion; e.g. 'He was a Protestant but he turned.'
WATTLE	'What will'; e.g. 'Wattle I do next?'

WERSH	Unsalted porridge.
WHEEK	Snatch abruptly away.
WHEEN	Small quantity but sometimes a good amount. e.g. 'He gave me a good wheen of carrots.'
WILE	Severe; e.g. 'The wind was wile strong last night.'
WISNAE	Was not; e.g. 'He said he wasnae comin'.'
WYER	Whether; e.g. 'I'm goin' wyer you like it or not.'
YILHAFTA	'You will be compelled to do so'; e.g. 'Yilhafta pay up.'

Also by John Pepper

WHAT A THING TO SAY

'I've a wheezle and I'm very durbley on my feet.' 'This oul tea's like cowl clart.' 'Him an' her's thick.' As John Pepper says, the visitor to Ulster might be forgiven for thinking there should be signs up at entry points to the province saying 'English *nearly* spoken here'. After reading *What a Thing To Say*, anyone who's asked 'Wherreryefir?' will be able to reply, 'Amferout,' just like one of the natives.

Paperback £1.75

D'YE MIND THE DAY

'Boiled lobsters for 6d', 'Bon-ton style straw hats for three-and-six', '25 million acres of virgin Canadian soil at 2/- an acre' — advertisements like these appeared in the *Belfast Telegraph* just a yesterday ago. So too did events great and small — Royal visits, two World Wars, the Depression, tragedies and triumphs. John Pepper, one of Northern Ireland's best-loved journalists, is the perfect companion through almost a century of news and pictures, accompanying his nostalgic selection with his own witty and informative commentary.

Paperback £2.50